I don't need my Pacifier Anymore

ILLUSTRATED BY
K.T. BAXTER

NOTES FOR PARENTS

There is no getting away from it, when you have a child who sucks their thumb, or indeed a pacifier; it's a hard habit to break. We've all fallen prey to bad habits, and I would like you to pause for a moment and just remind yourself how hard it was to break that habit. Maybe you had a bad habit of spending too much time on social media, of eating too many candy bars, of watching too much TV. You knew you had a bad habit, and even with your fully developed adult mind, it was a hard call to stop that repetitive behaviour. Why? Simple, because you *liked* candy, social media is fun and watching loads of TV at the end of the day was a good way for you to relax.

So firstly, give your child a break. Their minds are not fully developed, they *like* to suck their pacifiers, it makes them feel better and that's a hard habit to break. And after all it was something that you gave them.

The good news is that it is not impossible. However, it's a good idea from the start to focus on the positives. Telling your children that if they don't stop, they will end up with wonky bent teeth and they will look stupid in public, is not a good route to take.

The approach taken by this book is that sucking your pacifier is a right of passage and that your child can find restful sleep and comfort without sucking on it. Often pacifier sucking is a reaction, and children are not even aware that they are doing it.

The story is simple. Your child is going to choose a cuddly friend to take to bed to help them break the habit. This has been found to be useful, as holding a bear occupies the hands, and the story is designed to take your child off to sleep before they reach the end, ideally without a comforting thumb in their mouth.

Please do not expect instant results. There are different stories to listen to, all reinforcing the message that they can go to sleep without sucking their thumb and that their cuddly friend is there for reassurance, comfort and to help them find gentle peaceful and safe sleep.

There are a wide variety of other "tools" on the market to help with this problem, from awful tasting gels to put on thumbs, to gloves and even splints to keep a child's arm rigid so that they cannot reach their mouths with their hands. I am sure these do work but ask yourself what you would do if there was suddenly a lock on the refrigerator keeping you from the goodies you wanted to eat. What would you do? You'd find a way round it, break the lock, find the key, and persuade the key holder to just let you have one last cookie before they locked it again. So, my approach is very much to make this a decision the child wants to make and help them to realise that they can go to sleep and find comfort when they need to from within, without the need to suck on a thumb or a pacifier.

My Baby Days

My First Steps

My Toddler Days

Brushing my teeth at Bedtime

I will water him each day to make him grow

Made in the USA
Middletown, DE
16 December 2023

45856405R00015